9/06

W9-CBR-404

WARS THAT CHANGED AMERICAN HISTORY

America in World War II

Michael Burgan

WORLD ALMANAC® LIBRARY

Please visit our Web site at: www.garethstevens.com
For a free color catalog describing World Almanac® Library's list of high-quality books
and multimedia programs, call 1-800-848-2928 (USA) or 1-800-387-3178 (Canada).
World Almanac® Library's fax: (414) 332-3567

Library of Congress Catalog-in-Publication Data

Burgan, Michael.
  America in World War II / by Michael Burgan. — North American ed.
     p. cm — (Wars that changed American history)
  Includes bibliographical references and index.
  ISBN-10: 0-8368-7293-2 – ISBN-13: 978-0-8368-7293-4 (lib. bdg.)
  ISBN-10: 0-8368-7302-5 – ISBN-13: 978-0-8368-7302-3 (softcover)
  1. World War, 1939-1945—United States—Juvenile literature. I. Title.
II. Title: America in World War Two. III. Title: America in World War 2.
IV. Series.
  D769.B87   2007
  940.53'73—dc22   2006011846

First published in 2007 by
World Almanac® Library
A Member of the WRC Media Family of Companies
330 West Olive Street, Suite 100
Milwaukee, WI 53212 USA

A Creative Media Applications, Inc. Production
Design and Production: Alan Barnett, Inc.
Editor: Susan Madoff
Copy Editor: Laurie Lieb
Proofreader: Laurie Lieb and Donna Drybread
Indexer: Nara Wood
World Almanac® Library editorial direction: Mark J. Sachner
World Almanac® Library editor: Leifa Butrick
World Almanac® Library art direction: Tammy West
World Almanac® Library production: Jessica Morris and Robert L. Kraus

Picture credits: Hulton-Deutsch Collection/CORBIS: cover photo; Associated Press: pages 5, 6, 9, 10, 13, 15, 16, 18, 19,
20, 24, 25, 26, 28, 30, 31, 32, 33, 35, 37, 38, 39, 42, 43; maps courtesy of Ortelius Design

Printed in the United States of America

1 2 3 4 5 6 7 8 9 10 09 08 07 06

Table of Contents

Cover: U.S. soldiers watch from their landing craft the fighting already under way between German forces and the Allies in the Battle of Normandy. The massive D-day invasion took place on the coast of France on June 6, 1944, and remains the largest invasion by sea in military history, involving three million troops.

INTRODUCTION

From the time when America declared its independence in the 1700s to the present, every war in which Americans have fought has been a turning point in the nation's history. All of the major wars of American history have been bloody, and all of them have brought tragic loss of life. Some of them have been credited with great results, while others partly or entirely failed to achieve their goals. Some of them were widely supported; others were controversial and exposed deep divisions within the American people. None will ever be forgotten.

The American Revolution created a new type of nation based on the idea that the government should serve the people. As a result of the Mexican-American War, the young country expanded dramatically. Controversy over slavery in the new territory stoked the broader controversy between Northern and Southern states over the slavery issue and powers of state governments versus the federal government. When the slave states seceded, President Abraham Lincoln led the Union into a war against the Confederacy—the Civil War—that reunited a divided nation and ended slavery.

▼ Wars have shaped the history of the United States of America since the nation was founded in 1776. Conflict in this millennium continues to alter the decisions the government makes and the role the United States plays on the world stage.

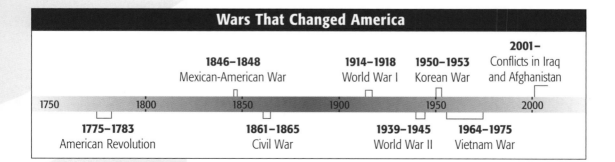

Wars That Changed America

1750	1800	1850	1900	1950	2000

1846–1848 Mexican-American War

1914–1918 World War I

1950–1953 Korean War

2001– Conflicts in Iraq and Afghanistan

1775–1783 American Revolution

1861–1865 Civil War

1939–1945 World War II

1964–1975 Vietnam War

The roles that the United States played in World War I and World War II helped transform the country into a major world power. In both these wars, the entry of the United States helped turn the tide of the war.

Later in the twentieth century, the United States engaged in a Cold War rivalry with the Soviet Union. During this time, the United States fought two wars to prevent the spread of communism. The Korean War essentially ended in a stalemate, and after years of combat in the Vietnam War, the United States withdrew. Both claimed great numbers of American lives, and following its defeat in Vietnam, the United States became more cautious in its use of military force.

That trend changed when the United States led the war that drove invading Iraqi forces from Kuwait in 1990. After the al-Qaeda terrorist attacks of September 11, 2001, the United States again led a war, this time against Afghanistan, which was sheltering al-Qaeda. About two years later, the United States led the invasion that toppled Iraq's dictatorship.

In this book, readers will learn about the largest and deadliest war in which the United States has participated. The war changed the world and divided the continent of Europe into geographical regions with two distinct and contrasting political ideologies. In Asia, the United States influenced change in Japan that led to the democratization of the country. The United States emerged from World War II as a world leader, with the military and diplomatic capabilities of the most powerful nation on earth.

▲ *U.S. Marines of the Twenty-eighth Regiment, Fifth Division, raise the American flag atop Mount Suribachi on Iwo Jima, an island in the Pacific located only 660 miles (1,062 kilometers) from Tokyo, Japan. Signaling a victory for the United States, the battle was one of the bloodiest of World War II. The photograph, taken by journalist Joe Rosenthal, caused an immediate sensation back home and resulted in the building of a national monument inscribed with the words "Uncommon Valor was a Common Virtue," located in Arlington, Virginia.*

CHAPTER 1

Roots of a War

On November 11, 1918, the battlefields of Europe rang with cheers. The war the soldiers were fighting was over. More than nine million soldiers had died, and whole villages had been destroyed. Now the world hoped for a lasting peace.

Around the world, people had called the conflict in Europe the Great War. When it ended, it was called the War to End All Wars. Almost three decades later, however, it would be called World War I, because another massive war followed it—World War II. The effects of these two wars lasted long after the battling nations signed peace treaties and sent their soldiers home. World War I drew the United States into world affairs as never before, and the country emerged with a new international status.

World War I began in 1914, but the United States did not enter it until 1917. Still, the United States played a key role in helping Great Britain and its **allies** defeat Germany and win the war.

President Woodrow Wilson had guided the United States through the war. Now Wilson hoped that the United States would play a major part in world affairs. He believed that promoting **democracy** around the world would help prevent future wars. Other U.S. presidents had welcomed the spread of democracy, but they had not actively worked to achieve it abroad. Most U.S. citizens were more interested in trading overseas than influencing foreign governments. Wilson, however, believed that creating new democracies would end the conflicts within nations that sometimes led to war. Democracies offered greater individual freedom than other forms of government, and people would be less likely to rise up against rulers they had elected. Democracies also favored free trade, which removed some of the competition between nations that could lead to war. Wilson thought that the United States had a moral duty to work for international peace, free trade, and personal freedom.

Even before the end of World War I, Wilson proposed his Fourteen Points, a plan to preserve peace and create democracies. Wilson called for creating a League of Nations whose members would work together to solve international problems before they led to war.

▲ A map of Europe in 1939 illustrates Czechoslovakia as a German-occupied territory. At the time, part of the German army was gathering in East Prussia in expectation of invading Poland. Germany would invade Poland in September, 1939. Although Hitler had an alliance with Italy's Mussolini as early as 1936, the Three Powers Pact creating the Axis powers was not signed until September 1940. The nations of Denmark, Norway, the Netherlands, Belgium, and France were occupied by German troops in 1940; Greece, Yugoslavia, Romania, Estonia, Latvia, Finland, and Lithuania would fall to Germany in 1941.

For example, if one country attacked another, League members would work together against the hostile nation. In some cases, Wilson said, that might mean using "the physical force of the world" to stop the invader, but he hoped that the League of Nations would never have to go war to keep world order.

Some Americans disliked Wilson's idea for the United States to join the League of Nations. These **isolationists** did not want the United States deeply involved in world affairs or dragged into future wars that did not directly threaten its safety. In the U.S. Senate, isolationist members prevented the country from joining the League. Most other major nations, however, joined the League when it began in 1920.

Changing Times around the World

Through the 1920s, the United States enjoyed a strong **economy**. As a whole, the country was rich, and most people who wanted jobs could find them. The decade was sometimes called "the Roaring Twenties." In 1929, however, the U.S. economy collapsed. Some people had bought stocks in companies as an investment. The price of the stocks rose as more people bought them, but these prices did not really reflect what the companies were worth. Investors thought prices would continue to rise, however, and that they would make money when they sold the stocks in the future. Some of the people buying stocks borrowed money to pay for them. At the same time, the U.S. economy was beginning to weaken. Companies could not sell all their goods, and prices for crops fell. To raise money, some people began to sell their stocks, making the value of the stocks fall. Other investors rushed to sell their stocks before the price fell further. This vast selling of stocks led to the stock market crash. Banks also began to

America in World War II

fail, and many people lost their life savings. A period known as the Great Depression soon began.

The Depression was felt around the world. In Germany, the economy was already weak because of the results of World War I. The European victors blamed Germany for starting the war. They had forced Germany to give up some of its land, destroy its weapons, and refrain from building new ones. Germany also had to pay **reparations** to the victorious European countries but had trouble finding money for these payments. The Depression added to the country's economic troubles.

During the 1920s, the United States loaned money to Germany so it could pay reparations. The stock market crash in the United States shut down the flow of money from U.S. banks to Germany and to nations that had borrowed from the United States during the war. In a sense, World War I had played an unexpected role in shaping the global economy.

The reparations and the tough economic times of the 1920s angered many Germans. They disliked the way the victors of World War I treated their country. Losing some of their land and their military forces made them feel weak. Many Germans were eager to accept the message of a new political leader: Adolf Hitler. During the 1920s, he had formed a political group called the Nazi Party. Its members wanted to restore Germany's place as a world power. Hitler wanted to rebuild the army and take control of European lands where Germans lived. As justification, he claimed that Germans were members of the Aryan race, a "master race" that was better than any

▲ *Many people went hungry during the Great Depression. In this 1933 photo, a group of jobless men in Cleveland, Ohio, line up to receive cabbages and potatoes from a relief agency.*

other race or ethnic group. In reality, no such Aryan race existed, but the idea of belonging to a master race fueled the Germans' pride. Hitler claimed that the Germans had a right to rule over other races and peoples, such as Jews, that he considered dangerous or weak.

The Rise of Tyrants

By 1933, Hitler and his Nazis had won the support of millions of Germans. That year, he was made chancellor, a key post in the German government. From that position, Hitler took control of the government. The Nazis clamped down on the freedom of the German population. They sent their political enemies and some Jews to special camps, called concentration camps, that were like prisons. In later years, some of these camps would become "death camps," where Hitler slaughtered millions of his enemies. Hitler also began to rebuild the German army, telling aides that his goal was "the restoration of the military strength of the German people." Other European nations protested, but they did not try to stop Hitler. By 1936, Germany had one of the most powerful militaries in the world. Two years later, Germany took control of Austria, a German-speaking nation to its south, and then the Sudetenland. This region of Czechoslovakia had many Germans in it, and Hitler claimed a right to rule it.

By this time, Hitler had formed an alliance with Benito Mussolini, the premier of Italy.

▼ In June 1933, German chancellor Adolf Hitler traveled to Italy to meet with Italian premier Benito Mussolini (right). In this picture, Hitler is greeted at the airport by Mussolini and an Italian honor guard.

America in World War II

He and Mussolini shared some political ideas and goals. Mussolini's Fascist Party had come to power in 1922. Like Hitler, Mussolini used force to silence his enemies and control the government. Also like Hitler, Mussolini sought to restore national pride and build an empire. In 1935, Italy invaded the African nation of Abyssinia (now called Ethiopia). Mussolini wanted revenge for a military defeat Italy had suffered there in 1896. He also saw the country as the first part of an Italian empire in Africa.

The Fascists in Italy and the Nazis in Germany were part of a wider movement in the 1930s. **Fascism** is a political philosophy that upholds the nation—and often race—as more important than the individual. Fascism calls for a strong central government headed by a dictator. Many countries at the time had fascist political parties, and Nazis were sometimes called fascists. In Germany, tens of thousands of people attended huge rallies in support of Nazi fascism.

A third nation was also seeking to build an empire at this time. Many of Japan's military leaders wanted to control the natural resources of other Asian nations. In 1931, Japan sent troops into a part of China called Manchuria. They set up a Chinese government there that followed Japan's orders. Six years later, Japan and China began a major war, and Japan quickly conquered a large part of central and northern China.

Facing a Growing Crisis

In 1932, U.S. citizens chose Franklin D. Roosevelt as their president. His major goal was to help people affected by the Great Depression. Most Americans and the lawmakers they elected remained isolationist. Starting in 1935, the U.S. Congress passed a series of laws designed to keep the United States neutral and out of other nations' conflicts.

The Spanish Civil War

In 1936, a civil war erupted in Spain. Italy and Germany supported Spanish fascists who opposed the elected government. Hitler sent the fascists some of his newest weapons to test how they worked during combat. Some Americans volunteered to help the Spanish government in the fight. Many of them joined a military unit called the Abraham Lincoln Brigade. By 1939, with German and Italian help, the Spanish fascists took control of their country. Spain remained neutral in World War II.

Fast Fact

In 1937, the Japanese committed horrible **atrocities** in the Chinese city of Nanjing (formerly known as Nanking). As many as 300,000 civilians were killed—some buried alive—and many buildings were destroyed. The fighting in Nanjing occurred at the start of the Sino-Japanese War and continued throughout World War II.

The Soviet Union

In 1918, **communists** seized control of the Russian government. The communists wanted the government to own all property and be run by just one political party— the Communist Party. The party limited free speech and political action. The Russian communists eventually created a new nation called the Soviet Union. In 1925, Joseph Stalin came to power. Over the next fifteen years, he killed 43 million people as he fought his enemies within the Soviet Union.

Adolf Hitler rejected communism because its belief that workers of all backgrounds were equal conflicted with his idea of a German master race. Still, Hitler thought it was in his interest to sign a treaty with Stalin. The agreement would give him time to take over the resources of Western Europe and then use them to achieve his long-term goal: the destruction of the Soviet Union and communism.

A few U.S. citizens, including Roosevelt, did not think the United States could stay out of the world's growing conflicts. The United States had an interest in protecting democratic allies that might come under attack. Another world war could also threaten U.S. economic interests overseas. At times, the president spoke out against threats to democracy and world peace. He wanted Americans to realize that isolationism might not always be a good option for the nation. Roosevelt knew, however, that most Americans still wanted to stay out of foreign wars.

The threat of a wider war grew in 1939. That spring, Hitler sent troops into the part of Czechoslovakia he did not already control. Germany also signed a nonaggression pact with the Soviet Union. In this treaty, the Germans and Soviets agreed not to attack each other. That promise meant that Hitler did not have to fear a Soviet invasion if Germany invaded more countries in Europe. Likewise, the Soviet Union could safely carry out its own planned military actions against neighboring countries without Germany stepping in. Privately, Hitler and Soviet leader Joseph Stalin also agreed to divide Poland between them. That Eastern European nation was the next target of Hitler's powerful military machine.

German forces invaded Poland on September 1, 1939. France and Great Britain both had treaties with Poland promising to help the Poles if their country were invaded. When Hitler refused to stop his invasion, Great Britain and France declared war on Germany. This was the beginning of World War II.

President Roosevelt declared that the United States would remain neutral. Soon, however, the country would be helping the Allies of Europe in their battle against Germany and preparing itself for a war that might come to its own shores.

America in World War II

CHAPTER 2

Giving Aid, Waging War

After taking control of Poland, Germany conquered Denmark and Norway by early 1940. Invasions of Belgium, Luxembourg, the Netherlands, and France soon followed. No country had an army strong enough to stop the German advance.

President Roosevelt and his supporters in Congress took small steps to help the Allies—at this time primarily France and Great Britain. In November 1939, Roosevelt convinced Congress to end a weapons **embargo.** The United States could now sell arms to countries at war, such as Great Britain and France. Roosevelt told the country, "There is a vast difference between keeping out of war and pretending that war is none of our business."

Roosevelt and the nation also kept an eye on Japan. During 1939, Japanese troops continued to march through China. The United States feared further Japanese advances in the Pacific, but was not prepared to go to war to stop them. Instead, the United States sent

▼ In 1937, during the second Sino-Japanese War, Japanese soldiers march into the Shansi province, attempting to secure part of the northern border of China. The Great Wall of China can be seen along the top of the photograph.

13

The Three Powers Pact

The agreement signed in Berlin, on September 27, 1940, by Germany, Italy, and Japan was called the Tripartite or Three Powers Pact. In it, Japan agreed that Germany and Italy would control Europe, while Germany and Italy recognized that Japan would control eastern Asia. The three nations agreed to help each other if "attacked by a power at present not involved in the European war or in the Chinese-Japanese conflict." The only major nation not yet involved in those wars was the United States.

The Three Powers sometimes used their capital cities when referring to themselves, calling their alliance the Berlin (Germany)-Rome (Italy)-Tokyo (Japan) Axis. Throughout World War II, the three nations were often called the Axis Powers.

Fast Fact

More than forty nations eventually received lend-lease aid, totaling more than $49 billion, from the United States. Some of this cost was eventually paid back when Allied nations provided U.S. troops abroad with aid and supplies.

aid to the Chinese and ended trade agreements with Japan. In 1940, the United States placed an embargo on steel and airplane fuel, two resources that the Japanese desperately needed and the U.S. had previously supplied. In response, Japan signed a treaty with Germany and Italy.

More U.S. Involvement

In Europe, Hitler sent waves of German planes to bomb Great Britain. President Roosevelt, meanwhile, kept looking for new ways to help the Allies. In August 1940, he arranged for a trade with Great Britain. In exchange for fifty U.S. ships, the British would let the U.S. Navy use some of their ports. Great Britain also bought weapons from the United States. As the war continued, however, the leader of the British government, Prime Minister Winston Churchill, warned that England would not be able to pay cash for the arms it needed to purchase in the very near future. In 1941, Congress approved a plan called lend-lease. Lend-lease allowed the president to aid any nation whose defense he believed was vital to the United States and to accept repayment "in kind or property, or any other direct or indirect benefit which the President deems satisfactory." Lend-lease, Roosevelt said, would strengthen the Allies in their fight against dictatorships. Defeating Germany, the president believed, was necessary to preserve what he called the "four freedoms" of democracy: freedom of the press, freedom of religion, freedom from want, and freedom from fear.

Although lend-lease was originally created to aid Great Britain in its war effort, the Soviet Union was accepting lend-lease aid by the end of 1941. In June that year, Hitler broke his agreement with Stalin and invaded the Soviet Union. Hitler wanted to acquire

America in World War II

the oil, coal, and other natural resources the Soviets controlled, as well as to destroy communism there. Many U.S. citizens disliked Stalin and his communist government because they opposed what Americans cherished—personal and economic freedom. Roosevelt, however, believed that helping the Soviets was the only way to defeat Hitler.

Soon after the German invasion of the Soviet Union, Roosevelt held his first wartime meeting with Winston Churchill. The two men signed what was called the Atlantic Charter. It outlined the long-range goals of the United States and Great Britain, which included defeating the Nazis and restoring peace in the world. Separate from the charter, Roosevelt also promised more help for Britain. Churchill later said that the president pledged to "wage war, but not declare it," and some historians have said that Roosevelt was willing to take steps that might lead to a German attack on the United States. Roosevelt would thus achieve his goal of getting the United States to fight in Europe—and Americans would finally accept entering the war.

One step was sending U.S. warships to protect British merchant ships carrying goods across the Atlantic Ocean. German submarines called U-boats were sinking many of the merchant ships before they reached Europe. Roosevelt knew that a U.S. ship might come under attack, but he accepted the risk, even if it meant bringing the United States into the

▲ *During a period known as the Blitz (1940–1941), Hitler's army bombed cities throughout the United Kingdom, hoping for their surrender. Following a bombing in London in January 1941, rescue workers search for survivors amid the wreckage of a building. Forty-three million people died in the Blitz.*

Fast Fact

In 1940, almost 15 percent of Americans who wanted jobs were out of work. Building weapons and other supplies for the Allies and the U.S. military created jobs and ended the Great Depression. By 1941, the number of jobless workers had fallen from 8 million to 5.5 million, and by the end of World War II, only about 1 million Americans who wanted jobs could not find them.

The Atlantic Charter

Here is part of the agreement made between Roosevelt and Churchill, released to the public on August 14, 1941.

[The United States and Great Britain] respect the right of all peoples to choose the form of government under which they will live.... After the final destruction of the Nazi tyranny, they hope to see established a peace which will afford to all nations the means of dwelling in safety within their own boundaries...[so] that all the men in all the lands may live out their lives in freedom from fear and want.

▶ The USS Arizona *burns in Pearl Harbor, Hawaii, on December 7, 1941, taking more than 80 percent of its fifteen hundred crew members with it. A surprise attack by the Japanese army in the early morning hours all but destroyed the U.S. Pacific Fleet and left more than three thousand Americans dead or missing. It was the first attack on U.S. territory since 1812.*

war. In October, a German submarine sank the USS *Reuben James*, but Congress still would not act.

The Japanese Attack

Through 1941, tensions also grew between Japan and the United States. Japan had benefited from Germany's victory in Europe. France and the Netherlands could not prevent Japan from taking control of their colonies in Asia. Japan also prepared to attack British colonies that were rich in natural resources, such as rubber and tin. In response, President Roosevelt froze Japanese funds held in U.S. banks and companies, so the Japanese could no longer use that money to buy goods. Roosevelt also tightened the embargo with Japan, which led to the end of almost all trade. The loss of American oil and gas was most damaging to Japan.

Diplomats tried to lessen the tensions between the two countries, but their militaries prepared for war. By the fall of 1941, Japan's leaders decided to attack the United States if the Americans refused to sell them oil. Japan knew that the United States was the

America in World War II

only nation powerful enough to stop it from invading more Asian lands. Japan wanted to strike first and weaken the U.S. forces in the Pacific that could be used against Japan in the future. By this time the United States had broken a secret code that Japan used to send messages to its diplomats. U.S. leaders knew that Japan planned to attack, but they did not know where or when.

The answer finally came on December 7, 1941. Early that morning, Japan attacked the U.S. Navy base at Pearl Harbor, Hawaii. Eight U.S. battleships—the largest, most powerful ships in the fleet—as well as other ships were docked there. For two hours, about 350 Japanese planes dropped bombs, launched torpedoes, and fired their guns at the U.S. ships and the planes and people on the ground. When the attack ended, twenty U.S. ships had been sunk or damaged, and more than 350 planes were damaged or destroyed. U.S troops had almost thirty-five hundred casualties, while the Japanese had few losses during their surprise attack.

On December 8, President Roosevelt asked Congress to declare war on Japan. He said that Americans would "defend themselves to the utmost" and "make it very certain that this form of treachery shall never endanger us again." He called December 7, the day of the attack on Pearl Harbor, "a date which will live in infamy." On December 11, Italy and Germany honored the Three Powers Pact by declaring war on the United States. Congress then voted to declare war on those two nations as well. The United States was now fully committed to helping Great Britain and the Soviet Union defeat Germany in Europe. At the same time, it took aim at Japan in Asia. World War II was now truly global.

Witness to Pearl Harbor

In December 1941, Daniel Inouye was a teenager living in Hawaii. He later became a U.S. senator. Here, Inouye describes what he and his family saw during the attack on Pearl Harbor: "We stood in the warm sunshine...and stared out toward Pearl Harbor. Black puffs of... smoke littered the pale sky... now the dirty gray smoke of a great fire billowed up over Pearl and [hid] the mountains and the horizon, and if we listened attentively we could hear the soft crrrump of the bombs and the hysterical chatter of the [antiaircraft guns]."

Fast Fact

Two weeks before the sinking of the *Reuben James*, a German U-boat attacked the USS *Kearny*, killing eleven sailors. They are sometimes considered the first American **casualties** of World War II. About one hundred Americans died when the *Reuben James* went down.

CHAPTER 3

War on Three Continents

A s 1941 ended, Hitler's Nazi forces dominated Europe. Great Britain did not have the men or equipment to invade the western half of the continent, which was called the Western Front. Germany directed its main forces against Russia, on the Eastern Front. In military terms, a front is where conflict or military actions takes place. Germany and Italy also held land in North Africa.

The United States worried about a direct Japanese attack on the U.S. mainland. After Pearl Harbor, one U.S. general in San Francisco warned, "Death and

► *Adolf Hitler (center) poses in front of the Eiffel Tower in Paris, France, in June 1940, one day after France surrendered to Germany. On the right is Arno Breker, Hitler's favorite sculptor, and on the left is Albert Speer, Hitler's chief architect. A cameraman filming the event can be seen in the foreground of the photograph.*

destruction are likely to come to this city at any moment." Japan, however, was more concerned about strengthening its control of East Asia. Japan still controlled large parts of China and several Pacific islands. In the hours after the Pearl Harbor raid, the Japanese also attacked other Pacific islands under U.S. control. Japan quickly seized Wake Island, where the United States had a small base. In late December, the Japanese invaded the Philippines.

Pacific Battles

At first U.S. and Filipino forces, under the command of General Douglas MacArthur, resisted the Japanese invaders, but by April 1942, the Japanese had smashed the U.S. troops. MacArthur fled to Australia, while the Japanese forced some 75,000 prisoners—mostly Filipinos—to walk to a prison camp 90 miles (145 kilometers) away. As many as fifteen thousand soldiers died on this Bataan Death March. The next month, Japan took Corregidor, an island near Bataan. All U.S. forces in the Philippines soon surrendered.

With its attack on Pearl Harbor, Japan had hoped to wipe out the U.S. fleet in the Pacific. The United States, however, still had its aircraft carriers, large ships used to launch planes at sea. In May, Japanese and U.S. carriers fought a major naval battle in the Coral Sea, east of New Guinea.

The Battle of the Coral Sea marked the first time that enemy ships fought without actually sailing close enough to see each other. Planes from each side's ships carried out the attack. The United States sank one small Japanese carrier and damaged a larger one. The Japanese sank the U.S. carrier *Lexington* and damaged the *Yorktown*. Neither side won a clear victory, though as one newspaper reported, Japan had "suffered her most severe setback of the war."

Douglas MacArthur

Douglas MacArthur (1880–1964), pictured here, was the son of an army officer who had fought in the Philippines during the Spanish-American War of 1898. MacArthur entered the army in 1903 and fought in World War I. Some Americans considered the general a hero for holding out so long against the larger Japanese army that invaded the Philippines. Others, however, thought his military decisions had hurt the U.S. efforts. After his defeat in the Philippines, MacArthur made a famous promise to return to the islands and drive out the Japanese. For the rest of the war, he commanded U.S. forces in the Pacific.

Cracking the Codes

Both the Axis Powers and the Allies sent their radio messages in code. The two sides could pick up each other's messages, but they could not understand them if they did not know the codes. Japan and Germany often changed their codes, but Allied code breakers were still able to crack them. The Allies' skill in breaking their enemies' codes led to some of their military victories, such as the one at Midway. The United States also had its own special code, based on the Navajo language. This language is spoken by few if any people who are not Navajo Indians. Navajo soldiers called "code talkers" served in the Pacific, sending and receiving messages. The Japanese never cracked this secret code.

▶ *Smoke rises from the USS* Yorktown *after a Japanese bomber hit the aircraft carrier in the Battle of Midway (June 1942) near Midway Island in the North Pacific off the northwestern coast of Hawaii.*

The First Victories

A month after the Battle of the Coral Sea, Japan planned to attack Midway, an island about 1,100 miles (1,770 km) west of Hawaii. The United States had a base there. As at Pearl Harbor, the U.S. learned about the attack before it happened. This time, however, they were ready, and they had a surprise of their own for the enemy. The Japanese thought that only one U.S. carrier was near Midway. In fact, three were sailing near the island, and their planes had plenty of firepower to bombard the Japanese fleet.

On June 4, 1942, Japanese planes left four aircraft carriers and headed for Midway. U.S. antiaircraft guns hit many of the attacking planes. Meanwhile, the planes on the U.S. carriers headed for the Japanese ships. Japan lost four of its six aircraft carriers, more than 250 planes, and some of its best pilots. The United States lost just one carrier. A Japanese naval officer later said that Midway was "the battle that doomed Japan." The United States now had more aircraft carriers in the Pacific than Japan, and U.S. shipyards, working at full capacity, were quickly building new planes and ships of all kinds.

America in World War II

Battling the Germans

Besides fighting Japan in what was called the Pacific Theater, President Roosevelt wanted the Allies to invade Europe as soon as possible. Forcing Germany to fight on two fronts—Russia and Western Europe—would wear down its troops. U.S. military leaders hoped to launch a major assault by April 1943. British leaders, however, wanted to wait. They did not think enough soldiers and supplies could be sent to Great Britain by then. They also feared losing territory in North Africa and Asia.

By the middle of 1942, Roosevelt saw that the United States would not take part in a major European **offensive** that year. Eager to battle Hitler and his forces, the president agreed to send U.S. troops to North Africa.

In November, U.S. troops began Operation Torch with an **amphibious** landing in Morocco and Algeria. Both of these colonies belonged to France. Since Germany's defeat of France, German forces had occupied northern France, while a French government called Vichy controlled French colonies and southern France. In reality, however, Vichy was a "puppet" government—it did what Germany demanded.

At first, French Vichy forces in Morocco and Algeria resisted the U.S. invasion. Soon, however, most of them agreed to join the Allies against Germany. Then, for the rest of 1942 and into the following year, the Allies battled the Germans in Tunisia, another French colony in North America. The German commander was Erwin Rommel. Known as the Desert Fox, he and his Afrika Korps had earlier won a series of victories against the British, relying mostly on tanks. By May 1943, however, they were forced to pull out of Tunisia. U.S. forces thus helped secure an Allied victory against the Axis.

The Holocaust

During 1942, the world received its first reports about terrible atrocities in German-held lands. Adolf Hitler had decided to kill all of Europe's Jews. This policy resulted from his **anti-Semitism**—the belief that Jews were a blight on humanity. In each country the Germans conquered, they rounded up Jews and sent them to concentration camps. A Jewish organization reported that by June 1942, one million Jews had already been slaughtered. The death camps remained open until 1945.

About six million Jews died during the war. As a single event of catastrophic proportions, the Nazis' persecution and killing of the Jews has come to be called the Holocaust. After the war, as Americans learned about the horrors of the death camps, they supported aid to the survivors. President Harry Truman also backed the creation of Israel as an independent nation for the world's Jews.

Many non-Jews were also killed at the death camps. It is estimated that another six million people, including Gypsies, Poles, communists, homosexuals, and people with disabilities also died as targeted enemies of Nazi Germany.

CHAPTER 4

Turning Points

While the United States and Britain fought in North Africa, Germany and the Soviet Union continued to battle on the Eastern Front. In November 1942, after fierce fighting, Germany and its allies took the Soviet city of Stalingrad (now called Volgograd). The Soviets launched a counterattack and during 1943 slowly regained some of the land they had lost to Germany. This success marked one of the first turning points for the Allies, and these gains would build in the years to come.

Stalin still wanted Roosevelt and Churchill to open a second front in Western Europe. Roosevelt agreed, but Churchill wanted the Allies to invade Italy first. Britain also thought it was more important to beat Hitler than to fight Japan in Asia. The Americans, however, continued to attack islands controlled by Japan. Their goal was to acquire airstrips in the Pacific from which to launch bombing raids on Japan.

Roosevelt's military chiefs saw that an invasion of Italy made sense. They came to accept the British argument that an invasion might take Italy out of the war and force

▼ *A soldier throws himself from the cockpit of his Grumman F6F Hellcat fighter to escape a fire that started when the gas tank from his plane skidded across the flight deck of the aircraft carrier USS Ticonderoga upon landing.*

Hitler to send his troops to fight the Allies there. Plus, the Allied forces that had been fighting in North Africa could be used for the Italian attack. In July 1943, those troops began crossing the Mediterranean Sea to Sicily. Within weeks, Italian fascists turned against Mussolini. They forced him out of power and then signed a peace treaty with the Allies in September. Italy also agreed to fight against Germany, but never had a chance to offer the Allies much aid. German troops in Italy took away the Italians' weapons, and tens of thousands of German soldiers soon arrived to control the country.

From Sicily, the Allies invaded the Italian mainland. Troops advanced northward from the southern tip of the country until they met heavy German defenses south of Rome. In January 1944, the Allies tried to get around the Germans by landing troops behind them, at Anzio near Rome. The Germans trapped the Allied troops at Anzio for months. By spring, however, the Allies drove back the Germans and in June freed Rome from German control. Although the Germans remained in northern Italy, the successful Allied advance in the south marked another important turning point in the war.

The Importance of New Technology

Throughout the war, the Allies relied on new technology to fight their enemies, both on the sea and in the air. Before the war started, scientists in several countries had developed **radar** as a method of detecting distant objects. Britain used radar to warn of German airplane raids. Radar also played an important role in the Battle of the Atlantic. After the United States entered the war, German submarines, traveling in small groups called wolf packs, destroyed many U.S. merchant ships. At first the U-boats attacked ships

Wartime Conferences

During World War II, the Allies made both military and diplomatic decisions at a series of conferences. In January 1943, Churchill and Roosevelt met in Casablanca, Morocco, where Roosevelt agreed to the British plan of invading Italy and delaying the major attack on the continent until 1944. Later in 1943, Roosevelt, Churchill, and Stalin—"the Big Three"— met in Tehran, Iran, to discuss the upcoming Allied invasion of France and other issues. Just before this conference, Churchill and Roosevelt met with Chiang Kai-shek in Cairo, Egypt. Chiang was one of the Chinese leaders battling Japan. Roosevelt promised Chiang more aid. The next meeting of the Big Three came at Yalta, a Soviet city, in February 1945. The leaders focused on postwar issues, including what to do with Germany once it was defeated.

The Guns at Anzio

At Anzio, Italy, the Germans used two huge guns mounted on railroad cars to bombard the Allies. Each **shell** fired from the guns weighed more than 500 pounds (227 kilograms). Allied soldiers nicknamed the guns "Anzio Annie" and "Anzio Express." Bill Mauldin was an American cartoonist traveling with the troops who depicted his soldier characters, Willie and Joe, fighting at Anzio. Mauldin said at Anzio, "There was no place…where enemy shells couldn't seek you out."

▶ *A map of the Pacific region illustrates locations of major battles fought in World War II, including Midway Island and Iwo Jima, and the cities of Nagasaki and Hiroshima, Japan, where the United States dropped atomic bombs. Although the Japanese controlled a large area of the Pacific (in green), they lacked the planes and ships to defend all the territory. The Allied advance westward across the Pacific Ocean is marked with blue arrows.*

close to the U.S. coast and in the Caribbean Sea. Later the U-boats pursued Allied ships on the open waters of the North Atlantic Ocean. Allied planes, however, increasingly used radar to detect the submarines. On ships, the Allies had a similar detection system called **sonar**, which used sound waves to locate the submarines when they were underwater. The Allied sonar and radar systems, which were more advanced than anything the Axis Powers had, helped the Allies sink the U-boats and win the Battle of the Atlantic—another turning point in the war. By 1944, the Germans had virtually stopped hunting for merchant ships heading to Europe.

Throughout the war, U.S. factories produced large numbers of ships and planes. Japanese and German plants could not match this huge production. U.S.

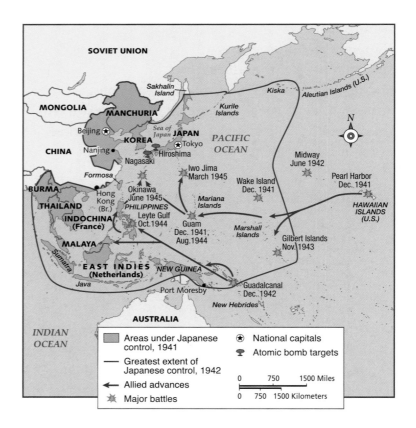

America in World War II

engineers also made important advances during the war. By 1944, some U.S. pilots were flying the "Hellcat." This fighter plane was faster than the best Japanese fighter and had more weapons. Some U.S. planes in the Pacific also carried improved radar.

The War Continues in the Pacific

Soon after the victory at Midway in June 1942, the United States won another key battle. U.S. officials learned that the Japanese were building an airstrip on Guadalcanal, one of the Solomon Islands. From this strip, Japanese planes would be able to attack ships traveling between Australia and the United States. In August 1942, eleven thousand U.S. Marines landed on the island and took control of the airstrip. Japanese troops, receiving supplies and **reinforcements** at night, spent more than six months trying to take it back. The U.S. Navy finally gained control of the waters off the island. By February 1943, all of Guadalcanal was under U.S. control.

Despite the U.S. success in the Pacific Theater, Churchill and Stalin still wanted the United States to focus on the war in Europe. Great Britain in particular favored merely defending against new Japanese attacks, rather than beginning large offensives. At the Casablanca conference, Churchill said, "When Hitler breaks down, all of the British resources... will be turned toward the defeat of Japan." U.S. military leaders, however, wanted to retake the Philippines and seize islands in the Central Pacific. The attack on Guadalcanal was part of that offensive strategy. The Allies attacked the Japanese on New Guinea and the Solomon Islands, then the Gilbert Islands and the Marshall Islands, in a slow drive toward Japan.

Fighting on Guadalcanal

J. R. Garrett was a U.S. Marine corporal at Guadalcanal. Here are his memories of the fighting there:

I remember seeing a big [Japanese] air raid come in and black anti-aircraft fire was coming crazy from all the [U.S.] ships in the harbor—all kind of puffs of smoke hit the sky.... Our planes were after them too. And way out there on the horizon, we saw the last one [Japanese plane] go down—all of them were shot down—we could see the fire and the smoke. These were big two-motor bombers: Japanese bombers burn real good.

Fast Fact

U.S. forces killed about twenty-five thousand Japanese troops on Guadalcanal, while losing about sixteen hundred U.S. soldiers.

CHAPTER 5

The U.S. Home Front

▼ *Buying war bonds was one way that U.S. citizens were able to support the war. In this photograph, a prize-winning cat is used to advertise and market the seventh War Loan Drive, which took place in New York City on May 15, 1945.*

During World War II, U.S. soldiers and sailors fought and died thousands of miles from home. Millions of young men left their hometowns—perhaps for the first time—and traveled to countries they perhaps had never even heard of before. They battled harsh living conditions as well as the Axis Powers. Ernie Pyle was a journalist who traveled with U.S. troops. He wrote how "tired and dirty soldiers" dealt with "smelly bedding rolls and... shirt collars greasy-black from months of wearing." Soldiers stationed overseas longed to see the friends and family they had left at another major scene of military action during the war—the home front.

Americans Do Their Part

World War II, like no other war before it, demanded tremendous effort from U.S. citizens who never picked up a gun. President Roosevelt said, "We must work and sacrifice" to help the soldiers fighting overseas. For civilians, daily life changed in many ways as soon as the United States entered the war. In January 1942, Congress passed a law that gave the government broad powers to limit the price of certain goods and services. At the same time, the government began to ration, or limit, the sale of certain goods needed for the war effort. Gasoline, rubber, sugar, shoes, and meat were all rationed.

The government also asked citizens to recycle certain goods so they could be turned into weapons. People stripped the metal bumpers off their cars and turned in pots and pans made of aluminum. Even the foil used to wrap gum was recycled, as were leftover cooking fats, which were used to make explosives. Americans helped finance the war effort by buying war bonds. The government promised to give buyers the amount they paid for the bond, plus extra money called interest, when the war ended. Advertisements in newspapers and magazines encouraged people to "Join the Fight" by buying bonds. Other government ads asked people to grow their own vegetables. The many "victory gardens" planted in backyards supplied about one-third of the country's vegetables.

The U.S. government also asked citizens to be prepared for possible enemy attacks. In cities along the East and West Coasts, officials held air raid drills. Citizens were taught to stay away from windows and to cover them with black curtains to block light from shining out, preventing the enemy from seeing possible targets. Civilians patrolled the coasts in private boats and airplanes, looking for enemy activity.

Changes in the Workplace

Even before Pearl Harbor, some U.S. industries had begun producing planes and other goods needed for war, both to help the Allies and to build up the U.S. military. After 1942, the country's largest companies

Espionage in New York

U.S. officials worried about German saboteurs—secret agents sent to destroy critical facilities such as factories, railways, or power plants. In June 1942, eight German saboteurs landed on the East Coast—four in Florida and four in New York. The four in New York ran into Coast Guard patrols, but they managed to hide some bombs on the beach and head into New York City. Within several days, however, the leader of the group turned himself in for fear of his punishment if he were apprehended. All eight saboteurs were soon caught. Historians do not know of any successful German saboteurs on U.S. soil.

Fast Fact

Nylon was invented in 1938 and soon was used to make women's stockings. During World War II, however, women could not buy nylon stockings because the materials were needed to make parachutes.

Women in the Military

During World War II, women also played an important role in the U.S. military. About 350,000 women volunteered for the armed forces. Some worked as nurses or performed military jobs away from the fighting. Jacqueline Cochran, pictured above, a pilot who flew in airplane races, suggested that the country use the skills of women like her. The government then created the Women's Airforce Service Pilots (WASPs). They flew planes to Europe and tested fighter planes at home. As one WASP later said, "We just wanted to do our part in the war effort." Several thousand women also joined the Office of Strategic Services (OSS), which was the country's first spy agency. These women sent and received codes, spread propaganda, and recruited spies to work for the United States.

began building huge amounts of military equipment. The Ford Motor Company opened a massive new plant that made bomber planes, and shipyards owned by Henry Kaiser were able to build one 440-foot-long (134-meter) "Liberty" cargo ship every five days.

The government encouraged women to take jobs inside the war plants, jobs that once belonged to the men now fighting the war. **Propaganda** posters announced that women's efforts would help the country win the war. Some women were also attracted by the high salaries they could earn in factories.

Women soon began building planes and other large items needed for the war. Metal bolts called rivets were used to build these items, and a famous poster celebrated "Rosie the Riveter," who represented all the women doing hard work to help the war effort. One of these women was Lucille Sunde, who worked at a shipyard. She said after the war, "A big sheet of metal was held up and we attacked with our rivet guns. I can still hear the sound ringing in my ears."

The film and music industries also took part in the war effort. Some entertainers joined the military and fought overseas. Civilian entertainers promoted the sale of war bonds and performed for troops overseas. Some movie stars stayed in Hollywood, the center of the film industry, and made motion pictures that served as both entertainment and propaganda. Some of these wartime films were *Casablanca, Sahara,* and *Mission to Moscow.*

World War II focused attention on relations between white and black Americans. For decades, African Americans had faced segregation at work, with many employers refusing to offer black workers good jobs or pay them the same wages as white workers received. The increased demand for workers in 1941 led to some improvements for African

America in World War II

Americans. President Roosevelt, responding to the demands of black leaders, ordered that industries making war goods could not discriminate against African Americans. Despite Roosevelt's order, however, many blacks continued to face discrimination at work. Still, the war gave many African Americans a chance to find good jobs in war plants.

Many African Americans moved from farms in the South to work in war plants in or near cities in the North, Midwest, and California. At times, relations between whites and blacks grew tense. In 1943, rumors spread through Detroit, Michigan, about alleged crimes committed by African Americans against whites and whites against African Americans. Riots broke out in the city, and thirty-four people—mostly African Americans—were killed. One observer noted that "on several occasions, persons running were shot in the back [by police].... In other instances, bystanders were clubbed by police."

Segregation and discrimination angered African Americans. During the war, many African Americans began to demand civil rights and equal treatment under the law. Activists created the Congress of Racial Equality, and membership in other civil rights groups grew tremendously. The efforts started during World War II fueled the larger Civil Rights Movement of the 1950s and 1960s.

Enemies at Home?

With the attack on Pearl Harbor, some U.S. leaders and citizens feared the presence of Japanese Americans in the country, especially on the West Coast, where there was a large number of residents of Japanese ancestry. People worried that Japanese Americans would try to help Japan by spying or becoming saboteurs. In 1942, President Roosevelt

African Americans in the Military

African Americans were particularly angry about the treatment of blacks in the U.S. military. During World War II, black and white soldiers were segregated in separate units, and most blacks were kept out of combat units. One black soldier wondered how the government could allow such discrimination and then expect black troops "to die for our country." (On July 26, 1948, President Truman desegregated the armed services.) Despite the prejudice they faced, African Americans played an important role in the U.S. armed forces during World War II. Just under one million served in the military. Some sailed on segregated ships that guarded **convoys** in the Atlantic. Others fought in Italy and the Pacific. Perhaps the most famous African American unit was the Tuskegee Airmen. The name came from the Tuskegee Institute, an African American university in Alabama where the soldiers trained as pilots and other crew members for bomber and fighter planes. The Tuskegee Airmen shot down more than 250 enemy planes during the war and won more than 860 medals for their bravery.

One Story of the Camps

In 2001, Norman Mineta became the head of the U.S. Department of Transportation. Almost sixty years earlier, he and his family had been forced from their California home to an internment camp in Cody, Wyoming. Here, he describes his arrival: "We arrived in the middle of a blinding snowstorm, five of us children in our California clothes. When we got to our tarpaper barracks, we found sand coming in through the walls, around the windows, up through the floors. The camp was surrounded by barbed wire."

▶ *Japanese Americans are readied to board a train that will take them from Santa Anita, California, to an internment camp in Gila River, Arizona.*

approved sending about 120,000 Japanese Americans to internment camps, also called relocation centers. In the process, these people lost most of their property and any businesses they owned. Some of the Japanese Americans were U.S. citizens, who were denied their legal rights by being forced out of their homes and sent to the camps.

The relocation centers were located in seven states, mostly in the West. Armed guards kept watch over the camps. The only way Japanese Americans could leave was to volunteer for the military. About eight thousand took this offer, joining all-Japanese units that fought bravely for the United States in Europe. One, the 442nd Regimental Combat Team, won more medals than any other fighting unit in U.S. history.

About eleven thousand German Americans and ten thousand Italian Americans were also sent to relocation camps. Some were citizens of Germany and Italy who happened to be in the United States when the war began. Others were American citizens who had lived in the United States for years.

Decisive Battles

For the Allies, the major goal of 1944 was beginning the fight along the Western Front in France. U.S. general Dwight D. Eisenhower chose to strike in Normandy, a region in northwest France, and called the Normandy invasion Operation Overlord. The Germans knew an invasion was coming, but they did not know exactly where. To confuse the Germans, the Allies used spies and radio messages to spread false information about the Allied plans. The messages included orders sent to an army that did not actually exist. The Allies even built a fake base for this imaginary army. These efforts convinced Germany that the main Allied invasion would come either in another part of France or in Norway.

▼ *A first wave of beach battalion Ducks lies low under the fire of Nazi guns on the beach of southern France on D-Day, June 6, 1944 during World War II. One invader operates a walkie talkie radio directing other landing craft to the safest spots for unloading their parties of fighting men.*

D-Day and Beyond

Eisenhower picked June 5 as D-day—the day of the invasion. Bad weather forced the Allies to wait until June 6. That morning, Allied **paratroopers** landed on the French coast, while Allied planes attacked German defenses. The big guns from Allied naval ships offshore fired away, and British, American,

Dwight D. Eisenhower

Dwight D. Eisenhower (1890–1969), pictured above, attended the U.S. Military Academy at West Point, New York. During World War I, he trained U.S. soldiers. After the war, he held a number of jobs, including a position as the first assistant to General Douglas MacArthur. When World War II began, Eisenhower was working for the U.S. Army while stationed in Washington, D.C. Soon, however, he was in England, commanding all the Allied forces in Western Europe. The Allied success with the Normandy invasion made Eisenhower a hero in the United States. He was elected president in 1952 and served for eight years.

Fast Fact

Before Operation Overlord, the United States sent soldiers, landing craft, planes, and supplies to Great Britain. The Allies eventually had 13,000 airplanes, 30,000 vehicles, 5,000 ships, and 150,000 soldiers ready for the amphibious attack.

and Canadian soldiers came ashore at five different beaches. The Germans were surprised by the assault, and Hitler was convinced that the Normandy invasion was just a **diversion**. For several hours, he refused to send reinforcements.

The German defenses were strongest at a strip of sand nicknamed Omaha Beach, which the U.S. troops attacked. They suffered almost three thousand casualties, but they took the beach, and the other four fell as well.

Aiding the Allies were members of the French Resistance and the French Forces of the Interior. These groups were made up of French citizens who wanted to defeat the Nazis. Across Europe and Asia, the British and Americans secretly worked with natives of the countries conquered by Germany and Japan. For the United States, the Office of Strategic Services led these efforts. After the war, many OSS members joined the Central Intelligence Agency (CIA), which still exists today. With OSS help, members of resistance movements in Europe acted as spies and saboteurs, weakening the Nazis.

The Allies now had the two-front war that Stalin had desperately wanted for so long. The Soviet Union was continuing to fight well in Eastern Europe. At the same time, Great Britain and the United States increased their bombing raids over Germany. U.S. pilots usually targeted factories producing military goods for the German war effort. By the end of 1943, the Allies had developed fighter planes that could fly far over Europe from their bases in Britain. These planes attacked the German fighters sent to shoot down Allied bombers. With better protection by their own fighters, the Allied bombers had better luck dropping their bombs and safely returning to their

America in World War II

bases. By the end of 1944, the Allies controlled the skies over northwestern Europe.

The Germans Strike Back

By September 1944, the Allies had pushed through Belgium and Luxembourg and sat near the German border, having rolled through France faster than Eisenhower had expected. The Allies' supply lines could not get enough fuel to the Allied tanks and other vehicles, so Eisenhower delayed moving into Germany.

This delay gave Germany time to strengthen its defenses and prepare for another counterattack. Hitler prepared to send about 500,000 men and more than one thousand tanks through the Ardennes, a Belgian forest that bordered Germany. He hoped to recapture Antwerp, a Belgian port, and split the British and U.S. forces approaching Germany.

The German assault, begun on December 16, 1944, surprised the Allies. The Germans were able to push back part of the Allies' front line, creating a bulge in it. This led to the American nickname for the German attack—the Battle of the Bulge. By December 22, the Germans had surrounded U.S. forces in the town of Bastogne. The German

◀ *Allied soldiers in winter camouflage gear transport supplies to the front lines during the Battle of the Bulge in the Ardennes region of Belgium on January 28, 1945.*

A Deadly "Wind"

During the naval battles off the Philippines, Japan began using a new weapon called the kamikaze ("divine wind"). The Japanese loaded bombs into planes that the pilots deliberately crashed into U.S. warships. The kamikaze pilots knew they would die on their mission. They took pride in knowing that their death would help Japan's war effort. In April 1945, one kamikaze pilot wrote in his diary, "It is the last time that I shall breathe the fresh air of the morning. Everything that I do today will be for the last time."

Kamikaze planes sank or badly damaged more than seventy U.S. ships.

commander sent a message to General Anthony C. McAuliffe, suggesting he surrender. McAuliffe had a brief reply: "NUTS!" General George Patton soon arrived to help the Allied soldiers at Bastogne. By the end of December, the Allies had halted the German advance in Belgium. Hitler decided to pull his troops back into Germany.

Return to the Philippines

In the Pacific, the United States continued to make gains against Japan. A little more than a week after D-day, U.S. Marines made an amphibious landing on Saipan in the Marianas Islands. Taking Saipan was key to the Allied plan of launching air attacks on Japan from island bases in the Pacific. During the fighting in the Marianas, U.S. and Japanese aircraft carriers fought their last major carrier-based battle. In this Battle of the Philippine Sea, Japan lost three carriers and about four hundred planes. The United States demonstrated superior strength in its training, battle technique, and air defense.

In October, General MacArthur began his long-planned invasion of the Philippines. Fulfilling the promise he had made in 1942, MacArthur told the Filipinos, "By the grace of Almighty God, our forces stand again on Philippine soil." In several days of combat, U.S. planes, ships, and submarines destroyed twenty-eight Japanese vessels. By the end of 1944, the Allies regained control of most of the Philippines.

While the Americans were retaking the Philippines, the British fought the Japanese in the British colony of Burma, which Japan had invaded in 1941. Chinese troops and U.S. forces operating out of China helped the British regain Burma. By the end of 1944, the Allies were tightening their grip on Japan, just as they were ending Hitler's control of Europe.

America in World War II

CHAPTER 7

Victory

In February 1945, U.S. president Franklin Roosevelt, Prime Minister Winston Churchill of Great Britain, and Soviet leader Joseph Stalin met at Yalta, in the Soviet Union. The Big Three were confident that the war in Europe would soon be over. By this time, Soviet troops were just 40 miles (64 km) west of Berlin, the German capital. On the Western Front, the Allies had continued their advance after fighting off the German counterattack in the Ardennes. The three leaders wanted to decide how to end the war in Europe. Stalin also agreed to join the war against Japan once Germany was defeated.

▼ British prime minister Winston Churchill, U.S. president Franklin D. Roosevelt, and Soviet premier Joseph Stalin (seated from left to right) are photographed at the Big Three conference in Yalta on February 12, 1945. The decisions made at the conference changed the map of Europe and made the Soviet Union the dominant power in Eastern Europe.

The New President

When President Roosevelt arrived at Yalta, he had just won his fourth term as president—more terms than any other president before or since. (The Twenty-second Amendment to the U.S. Constitution, ratified in 1951, prohibits any president from serving more than two terms.) Roosevelt, however, was a sick man. Heart trouble left him tired and weak, and he died just two months later. His vice president, Harry S. Truman, then became president and led the United States through the last months of the war. In some ways, Truman felt unprepared for the job, because, as vice president, he had not been deeply involved in making decisions regarding the war. He had to spend many nights studying secret messages he had never seen before, trying to understand Roosevelt's diplomacy and the position of U.S. troops. Truman needed to learn quickly, because he would have to make many important decisions in the months to come.

What to do with Germany after the war was a major issue. The Allies agreed to split the country into four zones, with each of the Big Three controlling one and France governing the fourth. Stalin also wanted reparations from Germany. Remembering what had happened after World War I, Roosevelt warned against demanding too much. He wanted to "leave Germany enough industry and work to prevent her from starving."

In general, Stalin got many of the things he wanted at the Yalta conference, especially the strong influence the Soviet Union would have in Eastern Europe after the war. Soviet troops already controlled most of the region, while the British and Americans had barely crossed into Germany. Stalin had the military power to get his own way.

Bloody Road to Victory

In early 1945, U.S. leaders were happy with Eisenhower's slow but steady push into Germany. He had agreed to massive bombing raids on German cities, such as Berlin and Dresden. The bombing killed many civilians, but Eisenhower hoped it would break the Germans' desire to fight, thus ending the war.

The Dresden raid was particularly deadly. The Allies dropped incendiary bombs—weapons designed to start huge fires. For two days, twelve hundred planes bombed the city, which sheltered many **refugees** trying to avoid the advancing Soviets. The fires that ripped through Dresden destroyed almost every building and killed as many as 100,000 people.

By this time, U.S. planes were also bombing cities in Japan from bases in the Marianas. In March 1945, the bombers dropped incendiary bombs on Tokyo. The raid was just as deadly as the one on Dresden. After completing their missions, some of the planes landed

America in World War II

on the tiny island of Iwo Jima. In the weeks before the Tokyo raid, U.S. Marines had fought a fierce battle to gain control of the island. About twenty-three thousand Japanese defenders were dug into trenches and caves when the U.S. troops landed on Iwo Jima. Both sides had high casualties, although Japan lost almost four times as many soldiers as the United States. Admiral Chester Nimitz later praised the "uncommon valor" that the Americans showed at Iwo Jima.

Back in Europe, the Allies continued to push across Germany. In April 1945, they were shocked at what they saw at the Nazi concentration camps. Earlier reports, Eisenhower said, did not truly describe the horrors of the worst of the death camps. Now he and others saw for themselves that Germany had imprisoned and killed millions of people, especially Jews. At the camps, the soldiers found mass graves of the dead. Many of the living looked like walking skeletons. These survivors, one reporter wrote, "hugged and embraced the American troops, kissed the ground before them...."

◀ *Two German soldiers are marched down a street followed by an armed U.S. soldier in Cologne, France, heading toward a prisoner-of-war camp behind Allied lines. An important railway hub, Cologne was taken by the First U.S. Army on March 3, 1945.*

Building a Bigger Bomb

The program to build the atomic bomb was called the Manhattan Project. At different sites across the United States, scientists in the program spent almost four years developing the deadliest weapon ever. The project was kept secret because Roosevelt and Churchill did not want Germany to learn about the work. They also did not want Stalin to discover the project, because they feared that one day the Soviet Union could threaten the United States and Great Britain. The British and Americans, however, did not know that the Soviets had spies working on the Manhattan Project. At Potsdam, Stalin knew the Americans had a working atomic bomb. The spies on the Manhattan Project later helped the Soviets develop their own nuclear weapon.

Later in April, U.S. and Soviet troops linked up at the Elbe River. Germany had now been invaded from the east and the west and had no hope of winning the war. On April 30, Adolf Hitler killed himself as Soviet tanks rolled through Berlin. A week later, Germany surrendered, and the war in Europe was over. President Truman noted that Americans had reason to rejoice, but warned that they should also remember "the terrible price we have paid to rid the world of Hitler."

The Bomb

After their victory in Europe, the Allies focused on ending the war in Asia. In July, Truman, Churchill, and Stalin met at Potsdam, in Germany. (During the conference, Clement Attlee replaced Churchill as prime minister of Great Britain.) Once again, Stalin talked about reparations. Truman, like Roosevelt, argued against them. Stalin also repeated his earlier statement that Soviet troops would now begin battling Japan.

At Potsdam, Truman learned that U.S. and British scientists had successfully tested a new weapon. The Allies had learned how to use the tremendous power stored inside certain **atoms** to create the most powerful bomb ever built. The Allies had once feared that Germany would build an atomic bomb before they did. Now, Truman knew he could use the bomb against Japan. He hoped the weapon would convince Japan to surrender, so the Allies would not have to invade Japan.

On July 28, China, Great Britain, and the United States asked Japan to surrender without any conditions, meaning that Japan would have to accept whatever decisions the Allies made after the war. Japan, however, refused to end the war on these terms. On August 6, a U.S. bomber flew high over the Japanese city of Hiroshima. The plane dropped an atomic bomb attached to a parachute, which slowed the bomb's fall so the plane could safely get away. Less than a minute later, the bomb exploded over Hiroshima, unleashing deadly **radiation**. Almost instantly, the blast from the "A-bomb" and the radiation killed about 80,000 people. Tens of thousands more died from wounds and radiation sickness in the months to come.

On August 8, the Soviets announced that they were entering the war against Japan. The next day, the United States dropped another atomic bomb, on the city of Nagasaki. Once again, there was instant death and destruction. Japan's emperor, Hirohito, decided that his country had suffered enough. On August 14, Japan agreed to surrender, not knowing that the United States did not have any A-bombs left. World War II would soon be over.

CHAPTER 8

Peace– and New Problems

▼ By 1955, Europe divided under the pressure of the Cold War. On one side were the Western nations, members of the North Atlantic Treaty Organization (NATO), while Central and Eastern European communist nations under the Soviet Union's influence belonged to the Warsaw Pact, created to combat the perceived threat from NATO.

In the United States and other Allied countries, people celebrated in the streets when they heard the war was over. In the months after Japan's surrender, millions of U.S. troops began returning home and leaving the military. They found a United States that had changed dramatically since 1941. The U.S. economy had grown tremendously during the war, ending the Great Depression. Despite some occasional tough times, the economy would continue to boom in the decades to come.

The U.S. government soon began programs to help the returning troops. Congress had already passed the GI Bill. This law paid for education and helped veterans get loans to buy homes or start businesses. Many ex-soldiers could not have gone to college without this aid. Returning soldiers also began to marry and start families, leading to what is now called the baby boom. Between 1946 and 1964, the men and women of the World War II generation had about 76 million children, known as baby boomers. Better education and jobs helped veterans

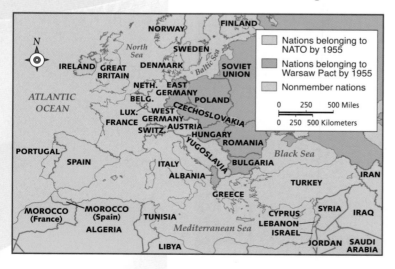

and their families buy homes in new suburbs that developed outside the nations' cities.

With the war over, the United States was now the most powerful country in the world. While other countries had been destroyed by war, U.S. factories buzzed with activity. They would provide the goods that both the Allies and the Axis Powers needed in order to rebuild.

Along with this economic might, the United States was now a military powerhouse. It alone had the capability to build atomic weapons, and its troops were stationed all over the world. These troops would help the United States carry out its postwar goals—sell goods, keep the peace, and spread democracy. In October 1945, President Truman said the United States had "no objective which need clash with the peaceful aims of any other nation."

A New Kind of War

Truman named General MacArthur as the military governor in Japan. MacArthur set up a democratic government while the United States helped its former enemy rebuild. Germany was split into four zones, as the Allies had earlier agreed. Both the defeated nations had been badly bombed, and many people lived in ruined cities. Ella Barowsky, a resident of Berlin at the time, recalled that even "the trees in the zoo were nearly all taken down [for firewood].... It was also incredibly difficult to get hold of food."

As 1945 came to an end, the United States and the Soviet Union began to argue about what should happen in Germany and Eastern Europe. The Soviets still wanted Germany to pay reparations. When they could not get money from the Germans, the Soviets took goods instead. Soviet soldiers took apart German factories and sent the equipment back to the Soviet

Television

World War II slowed the development of a new form of communication: television. The first electronic televisions were built during the 1920s. Many Americans saw a television for the first time in 1939 at the World's Fair in New York. During the war, however, inventors and scientists were encouraged to put all their time and energy into the war effort. After the war was over, the television industry grew quickly. Americans began buying TVs to watch shows that large companies sponsored as a form of advertisement. In 1946, only about twenty thousand U.S. homes had televisions. By 1950, the number had leaped to about 3.8 million.

Fast Fact

During World War II, more than 400,000 U.S. troops were killed, including deaths by accident and disease.

Union. Truman was not willing to give the Soviet Union complete control of Eastern Europe, even though its troops were still there. Soviet troops were also stationed in Manchuria, a part of China, and the northern half of Korea. Truman and his advisers knew that Stalin was creating communist governments in Eastern Europe and would try to help communists in Asia. The Americans wanted to create democratic governments that would share U.S. interests.

Although the Soviet Union had suffered terrible destruction during the war, it still had a large military. The Soviets posed the only threat to U.S. plans. Stalin feared a future attack from the West, so he wanted governments in Eastern Europe that took orders from him. Communists also believed they had a duty to spread their form of government around the world. They saw **capitalist** countries, such as the United States, as their main enemy. U.S. and Soviet leaders distrusted each other. Americans' fear grew after 1949, when the Soviet Union succeeded in building atomic weapons.

▼ General George S. Patton is cheered by thousands during a victory parade in Los Angeles, California, on June 9, 1945. Shortly after the war, Patton was relieved of his battle command post. He died of injuries from an automobile accident in Germany on December 21, 1945.

America in World War II

The United States and the Soviet Union had been forced to work together to defeat Hitler. Now, the former allies became enemies in what was soon called the Cold War. It was "cold" because the two sides never fought directly. Instead, they gave money and arms to other nations, which sometimes battled each other. At times, U.S. soldiers fought communists who were aided by the Soviets, as in Korea and Vietnam. A "hot" war, however, with the Soviet army fighting the U.S. army, never happened.

World War II caused great changes in the United States and in the country's role in the world. At home, women and African Americans played a larger role in the economy than ever before. They would begin to assert themselves even more in the years to come, demanding their full civil and political rights. The size of the government also expanded, as Roosevelt and Truman called on Americans to sacrifice for the war effort and build a military strong enough to win a war that spread out across the world.

As the most powerful of the victorious Allies, the United States threw aside its history of isolationism once and for all. Some Americans might complain about U.S. involvement overseas, but most political leaders believed that the country had a duty to confront tyrants such as Hitler. The U.S military was now the best equipped in the world, and the United States was willing to use that strength to pursue its interests, which included promoting free trade and democracy. Although the United States joined the United Nations, U.S. leaders thought they sometimes had a right to act on their own to settle regional land global problems. The United States, as Harry Truman said, had become a "giant," both feared and respected around the world.

The United Nations

During World War II, Franklin Roosevelt urged the Allies to create a new international organization called the United Nations (UN). He hoped that every country would send representatives and work together to prevent future wars. In April 1945, fifty nations met in San Francisco to plan the UN, and it was officially created that October. Now based in New York City, the United Nations has more than 190 members.

Fast Fact

As many as 27 million Soviet citizens died during World War II, from fighting, starvation, and disease. Some were killed by their own government; Soviet leaders harshly punished anyone who supported the Germans. The Soviet government feared that these citizens would be "infected" by Nazi ideas and seek to destroy communism.

TIME LINE

1918	The Allies defeat Germany in World War I.
1925	Joseph Stalin emerges as the leader of the Soviet Union.
1929	The U.S. stock market crashes, leading to the Great Depression.
1931	Japan takes over Manchuria, a region in China.
1932	Franklin Delano Roosevelt is elected president of the United States.
1933	Adolf Hitler comes to power in Germany.
1935	Italy invades Abyssinia (Ethiopia). U.S. Congress passes neutrality laws.
1936	Germany and Italy aid Spanish fascists fighting the elected government of Spain.
1937	Japan launches a major invasion of China.
1938	Germany takes control of the Sudetenland, a region in Czechoslovakia.
1939	March: Germany seizes the rest of Czechoslovakia; August 23: Hitler and Stalin agree not to attack each other; September 1: Germany invades Poland, beginning World War II.
1940	April–July: Germany rolls through western Europe and begins bombing Great Britain; September 27: Germany, Italy, and Japan sign the Three Powers Pact.
1941	June 22: Germany invades the Soviet Union; Congress passes Lend-Lease Act; August 14: Great Britain and the United States issue the Atlantic Charter; December 7: Japan bombs Pearl Harbor, bringing the United States into World War II.
1942	April: Japanese Americans are sent to internment camps; May: U.S. forces flee the Philippines; May 7–8: the United States and Japan each lose an aircraft carrier during the Battle of the Coral Sea; June 4–6: the United States wins its first major battle in the Pacific at Midway; November: U.S. forces arrive in North Africa.
1943	February: U.S. forces take control of Guadalcanal; July: Allied forces invade Italy; November 28: Stalin, Churchill, and Roosevelt meet in Tehran; Allied forces gain control of the Atlantic.
1944	June 6: The Allies invade France; June 13: Congress passes the GI Bill; June 19–20: the Allies win the Battle of the Philippine Sea; July: U.S. forces take control of Saipan; October: Allied forces land in the Philippines; December: Allied forces hold off a massive German counterattack at the Battle of the Bulge.
1945	February: Stalin, Churchill, and Roosevelt meet in Yalta; February–March: Allied planes firebomb Dresden and Tokyo; April 12: Roosevelt dies; Harry Truman becomes president; April 15: Allies enter German concentration camps; April 30: Hitler kills himself; Germany surrenders a week later; July: Stalin, Churchill, and Truman meet in Potsdam; August 6, 9: the United States drops atomic bombs on Hiroshima and Nagasaki; August 14: Japan surrenders, ending World War II.

GLOSSARY

allies friends and supporters of a person or country; when capitalized, refers to the United States and its allies during all wars

amphibious term applied to a land invasion that uses soldiers based on ships

anti-Semitism intense hatred and unfair treatment of Jewish people

atoms extremely small particles of matter that make up all substances

atrocities horrible acts of violence, often committed against civilians

capitalist a person who supports an economic system in which people or groups have the right to own private property and start businesses

casualties soldiers who are killed, wounded, missing, or taken prisoner during a battle

communists people who believe in a political system featuring one party that holds complete power and promotes government ownership of businesses

convoys groups of ships that travel together for protection

democracy a government ruled by the citizens of a state, either by directly voting on issues or electing leaders to represent their interests

diplomats government representatives who conduct negotiations between foreign countries

diversion an action or event that directs attention away from a more important action or event

economy the total goods and services produced in a country

embargo a government restriction on trading certain goods

fascism government by a central authority or dictator

isolationists people who do not want their nation to become involved in the affairs of other nations

offensive a military attack to gain ground

paratroopers soldiers who use parachutes to jump from planes

propaganda information spread by a government or group to influence people's thoughts, actions, or attitudes

radar a method or device that detects distant objects in the air or on the ground using radio waves

radiation a form of energy that can be deadly in large doses

refugees people forced to flee their homeland because of war or natural disaster

reinforcements extra troops sent to help an army

reparations money given by a defeated country after a war to pay for property that it destroyed

shell an explosive fired from large guns

sonar a method or device that detects objects underwater using sound waves

FOR FURTHER INFORMATION

Books

Altman, Linda Jacobs. *Hitler's Rise to Power and the Holocaust.* Enslow, 2003.

Britton, Tamara L. *Pearl Harbor.* Abdo, 2003.

Crewe, Sabrina. *The Atom Bomb Project.* Gareth Stevens, 2005.

De Capua, Sarah. *The Tuskegee Airmen: African-American Pilots of World War II.* Child's World, 2004.

Levy, Patricia. *The Home Front in World War II.* Raintree, 2004.

Platt, Richard. *D-Day Landings: The Story of the Allied Invasion.* DK Publishing, 2004.

Stanley, George Edward. *The Great Depression and World War II, 1929–1949.* World Almanac Library, 2005.

Web Sites

Franklin D. Roosevelt Presidential Library and Museum
www.fdrlibrary.marist.edu/

Harry S. Truman Presidential Library and Museum *www.trumanlibrary.org/*

Japanese American Relocation Digital Archives *jarda.cdlib.org/*

Multimedia Learning Center: World War II
motlc.learningcenter.wiesenthal.org/

Operation Overlord *www.eisenhower.archives.gov/dday.htm*

Rosie the Riveter: Women Working During World War II
www.nps.gov/pwro/collection/website/home.htm

Publisher's note to educators and parents: Our editors have carefully reviewed these Web sites to ensure that they are suitable for children. Many Web sites change frequently, however, and we cannot guarantee that a site's future contents will continue to meet our high standards of quality and educational value. Be advised that children should be closely supervised whenever they access the Internet.

INDEX

About the Author

As an editor at *Weekly Reader* for six years, Michael Burgan created educational material for an interactive online service and wrote on current events. Now a freelance author, he has written more than ninety books for children and young adults, including books on science, historical events, and great Americans. Burgan has a B.A. in history from the University of Connecticut. He resides in Chicago.